I'm the Chef!

I'm the Chef!

Crabtree Publishing Company

PMB 16A, 350 Fifth Avenue
Suite 3308, New York, NY
10118

612 Welland Avenue,
St. Catharines, Ontario
Canada L2M 5V6

Created by **McRae Books**

Coordinating Editor: Ellen Rodger
Project Editor: John Crossingham
Production Coordinator: Rosie Gowsell
Production Assistance: Mary-Anne Luzba
Consulting Chef: Dan Fudge

McRae Books Srl.
Writer: Karen Ward
Editor: Anne McRae
Photography: Marco Lanza, Walter Mericchi
Set Design: Rosalba Gioffrè
Design: Marco Nardi
Layout and cutouts: Giovanni Mattioli, Adriano Nardi, Laura Ottina
Special thanks to: Bartolini Dino (Florence) and Mastrociliegia (Fiesole) for their assistance during the production of this book.
Color separations: Fotolito Toscana, Florence, Italy

CATALOGING-IN-PUBLICATION DATA

Ward, Karen, 1968-
    The young chef's Mexican cookbook / Karen Ward.
      p. cm. -- (I'm the chef)
    Includes index.
    ISBN 0-7787-0281-2 (RLB) -- ISBN 0-7787-0295-2 (pbk.)
    1. Cookery, Mexican--Juvenile literature. 2. Quick and easy
cookery--Juvenile literature. [1. Cookery, Mexican.]   I. Title.
II. Series.
    TX716.M4W368 2001
    641.5872--dc21

2001017293
LC

123456789
Printed and bound in Italy by Nuova GEP, Cremona
987654321

I'm the Chef!

THE YOUNG CHEF'S
MEXICAN
COOKBOOK

Crabtree
www.crabtreebooks.com

List of Contents

Introduction

Centuries ago, Mexico was home to native people such as the **Aztecs** and **Mayans**. These people made dishes using corn, chilies, and cocoa beans. When European settlers arrived in Mexico, they brought different styles of cooking. Today, Mexican food is a mixture of Spanish, French, Italian, and Native American recipes. Corn, chilies, tomatoes, beans, peppers, and avocados are all basic ingredients in Mexican cooking. The 15 recipes in this book are some of the most common dishes. Step-by-step photographs help to explain each recipe. So enjoy, or as the Mexicans say, *"Del eitarse!"*

Chilaquilles

Tortillas and eggs

This dish is served for breakfast. Tortillas, the bread of Mexico, are made from corn or wheat. Sometimes chilaquilles are made without vegetables. You can impress your family by telling them that chilaquilles are *"una buena manera de empezar el dia,"* which is Spanish for "a good way to start the day."

1 Place one tortilla on the cutting board. Using a knife, cut it into bite size pieces. Do this for all six tortillas. Now peel the skin off of the onion. Chop the onion, tomato, and bell pepper into small pieces.

2 Break all the eggs into a bowl. Add the salt and pepper to the eggs. Use a fork or whisk to **beat** the eggs until they are **frothy**. Set them aside for later use.

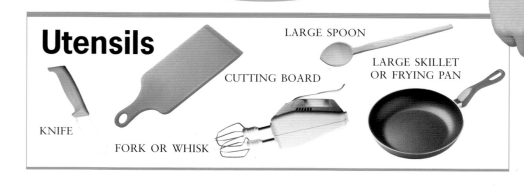

Utensils

LARGE SPOON

CUTTING BOARD

LARGE SKILLET OR FRYING PAN

KNIFE

FORK OR WHISK

3 Place a large frying pan on the stove. Turn the temperature to medium heat. Add half the vegetable oil. Wait one minute and add the onion and tortillas. Cook and stir until the onion and tortillas brown slightly. Add the remaining oil. Raise the temperature to medium hot. Wait a minute until the oil is hot, then add the peppers. Wait another minute and add the tomatoes.

4 Stir and cook until the vegetables are soft and the tortillas are light golden brown and crispy. Add the egg mixture and continue stirring until the eggs are cooked. Serve right away!

TIPS & TRICKS

Hot oil can splatter and burn. Be careful when adding food to the frying pan. Hold the plate with the food just above the pan. Use the wooden spoon to slip the food into the pan so that none of the oil splatters onto your hands. When stirring the food, hold the pan handle firmly with your other hand.

Ingredients

6 small corn tortillas

1 small onion, chopped

1 small tomato, chopped

1 bell pepper, chopped

6 eggs

1 teaspoon (5ml) salt

1 teaspoon (5ml) pepper

2 tablespoons (30ml) vegetable oil

Atole

Corn drink

Early Mexican farmers first grew corn over 5,000 years ago. These people called corn *toconayo*, which means "our meat," and many of them believed that the gods had created people from corn. Today it is used to make tortillas, **tamales**, and other breads. People even drink it! This recipe for *atole* is flavored with cinnamon and sugar, but you can add crushed fruit, spices, or other flavors.

1 Mix the cornstarch and water in a small bowl. Stir well until the cornstarch **dissolves** into the water. Set the mixture aside.

2 Pour the milk into a large pot and cook over low heat until it **simmers**. Stir often so that it does not burn. Once the milk is simmering, stir the cornstarch and water mixture again, and add it to the pot. Stir the contents of the pot and remove it from the stove.

TIPS & TRICKS

Before cooking, remember to ask an adult for permission and to wash your hands. When heating the milk for this recipe be careful. Milk starts to boil very quickly. Watch the pot and take it off the stove immediately if the milk starts to boil over.

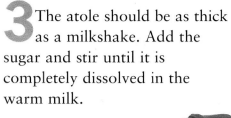

3 The atole should be as thick as a milkshake. Add the sugar and stir until it is completely dissolved in the warm milk.

4 Sprinkle cinnamon into the atole and stir well. Pour the atole into cups or bowls and serve.

Ingredients

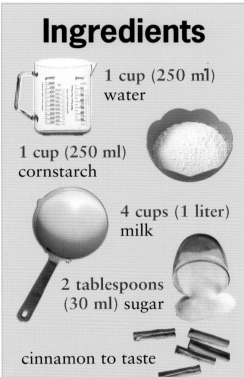

1 cup (250 ml) water

1 cup (250 ml) cornstarch

4 cups (1 liter) milk

2 tablespoons (30 ml) sugar

cinnamon to taste

Utensils

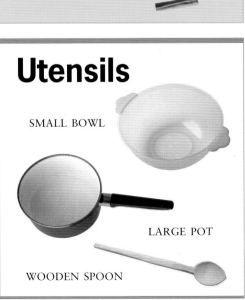

SMALL BOWL

LARGE POT

WOODEN SPOON

Chocolate Mexicano

Mexican hot chocolate

Chocolate originally came from Mexico. It is made from the beans of the cocoa tree which the Aztecs used in their cooking. When Spanish explorer Hernán Cortés met the Aztec ruler Montezuma in 1519, he was served a bitter cocoa drink called *xocoatl*. Cortés then introduced this drink to Spain.

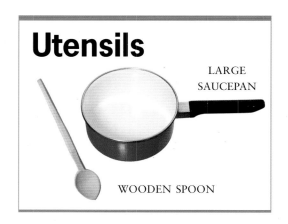

Utensils

LARGE SAUCEPAN

WOODEN SPOON

1 Place the sugar, cocoa, salt, flour, cinnamon, and water in a large saucepan. Place the saucepan over low heat and stir until the mixture dissolves into the water.

*For a quick and easy version of this recipe, follow these instructions: In a pot, boil 4 cups (1 liter) of milk. Add one tablet of **Abuelita Chocolate**. Stir until the tablet dissolves in the milk. Sprinkle with cinnamon and serve hot.*

2 After the mixture is dissolved, turn up the temperature of the stove to medium high. Stir the mixture until it boils. Boil for 3 to 5 minutes, stirring all the time.

3 Add the milk. Continue to stir until the milk is hot, but not boiling.

4 Just before the milk boils, remove the saucepan from the heat. Stir in the vanilla extract, and serve!

TIPS & TRICKS

Before you start to cook any meal, read the recipe through at least once. Check that you have everything that you need. You do not want to start cooking if you are missing any ingredients or utensils. Ask an adult to help you prepare.

Ingredients

½ cup (125 ml) sugar

¼ cup (60 ml) cocoa

¼ teaspoon (1 ml) salt

1 tablespoon (15 ml) plain flour

1 teaspoon (5 ml) cinnamon

1 cup (250 ml) cold water

4 cups (1 liter) milk

2 teaspoons (10 ml) vanilla extract

Sopa de tortilla

Tortilla soup

Sopa de tortilla is a classic Mexican soup. There are two types of soups. *Sopas secas*, or dry soups, are full of rice or noodles that soak up the **broth**, or liquid, while they are cooking. *Sopas aguadas*, or wet soups, are the soups that Americans and Canadians usually eat. *Sopa de tortilla* is a wet soup made with chicken stock. Make the chicken stock beforehand by adding a chicken stock cube to boiling water and stir until it dissolves.

1 Chop the onion, garlic, celery, and zucchini into small pieces.

2 Warm a saucepan over medium heat. Once the saucepan is hot, add the oil and vegetables to it. Cook until the vegetables are soft.

TIPS & TRICKS

It is usually best to do all the cutting and chopping before you begin cooking. Then you will have everything ready when you need it. When chopping ingredients, try to cut them all about the same size. This technique allows the pieces to be cooked evenly.

Utensils

KNIFE

LARGE SAUCEPAN

CUTTING BOARD

WOODEN SPOON

Ingredients

½ onion

2 cloves garlic

1 stalk celery, chopped

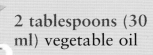
2 small zucchini

2 tablespoons (30 ml) vegetable oil

1 can tomatoes (13 oz/400 ml) or

2 cups (500 ml) crushed tomatoes

1 cup (250 ml) water

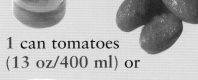
2 cups (500 ml) chicken stock

1 cup (250 ml) cooked corn

½ teaspoon (3 ml) cumin

corn tortilla strips or chips

1 avocado

3 Add all the other ingredients, except the avocado and tortilla strips. Stir often and simmer over low heat for 30 minutes.

4 When you are ready to serve, slice the avocado. **Ladle**, or scoop, the soup into individual bowls. Add some avocado and chips to each one, and serve.

Caldito

Beef and potato soup

Caldito is a healthy soup that the Mexicans say tastes *"Mejon en la manana!"* or "Better the next day!" This is an ideal dish if you are planning to invite friends for a Mexican meal and have a number of recipes to prepare. Make *caldito* the day before and just reheat it before serving. *Caldito* is a hearty soup and is perfect for winter evenings. As an extra touch, try adding some sliced green onions right before serving.

Utensils

LARGE SKILLET
OR FRYING PAN

KNIFE

CUTTING BOARD

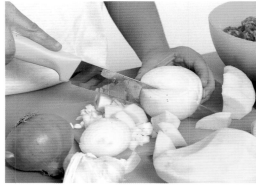

1 Chop the onion and fresh chilies (if you are using them instead of canned chilies). **Mince** the garlic, and **dice** the potatoes.

2 Place the beef, onion, potatoes, and garlic in a large frying pan over medium heat. Stir and cook until the meat is browned. Make sure there is no pink left in the meat. Drain any liquid that has formed in the pan. Ask an adult to help you. Remember the pan will be heavy and hot!

4 Add the water or chicken stock and stir well.

5 Add the green chilies and stir. Simmer over low heat for 30 minutes.

3 Return the meat mixture to the pan. The stove should remain at medium heat. Stir fry until the potatoes start to soften.

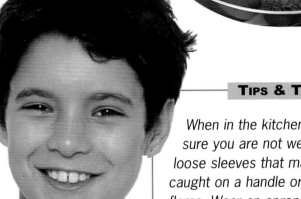

Ingredients

½ medium red onion, chopped

2 cloves garlic, minced

5 medium potatoes, diced

1 lb (450 g) ground beef

2 small cans chopped green chili or 8 to 10 fresh chilies, roasted, peeled, **veined**, and seeded

3 cups (750 ml) water or chicken stock

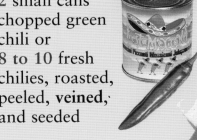

TIPS & TRICKS

When in the kitchen, make sure you are not wearing long, loose sleeves that may get caught on a handle or near a flame. Wear an apron to protect your clothes. Before opening canned items, rinse the tops to remove any dust sitting on top.

6 The next day, reheat and serve hot with tortillas

Guacamole

Avocado dip

Guacamole is a dip made of mashed avocados. It is flavored with chilies and lime or lemon juice, and often has chopped tomatoes, green onion, and **cilantro**. The word *"guacamole"* comes from two Aztec words—*"agucate"* meaning "avocado," and *"mole"* meaning "mixture." Some Mexican cities have their own way of serving *guacamole*. In Monterrey, the tomatoes and onions are served as a **garnish**, so that the dish looks like the red, white, and green stripes on the Mexican flag.

1 Cut the avocados in half lengthwise. Remove the stones.

2 Use a spoon to hollow out the green, fleshy part of the avocados. Put the flesh into the bowl.

TIPS & TRICKS

Many recipes in this book involve the use of a sharp knife for chopping and cutting ingredients. Take care when choosing the right knife. Talk to an adult about which is the best and safest knife in your kitchen for each job. When using a knife, hold it firmly in one hand and hold the ingredient in the other. Be sure that your fingers are well away from the blade.

3 Mash the avocado flesh using the back part of a fork. Add the lemon juice and salt. Stir.

4 Chop the green onion and the green chili. Peel and mince the garlic. Add the onion, garlic, and chilies to the avocado and stir well.

Utensils

BOWL

CUTTING BOARD

KNIFE

5 Chop the tomato into small pieces. Add the pieces to the avocado and stir well.

6 Place the guacamole in an attractive serving dish. Serve with **tostados** or corn chips as a dip.

Ingredients

2 avocados

½ teaspoon (2 ml) salt

2 teaspoons (10 ml) lemon or lime juice

½ tomato

2 cloves garlic

1 green onion

2 tablespoons (30 ml) green chili

Salsa pico do gallo

Mexican sauce

"Caliente!" means "hot!" That is the best way to describe this famous sauce. *Salsa* is a mixture of tomatoes, onions, chilies, and other ingredients. *Salsa* is served all over Mexico with tortillas and grilled meats, fish, or rice. It is also a popular appetizer and is served with a bowl of tortilla chips. This dish is best made during the hot summer months, when tomatoes are ripe.

The inside veins and seeds of a jalapeno are very hot. If you have them, use rubber gloves when chopping jalapeno peppers. Make sure you do not rub your eyes, and wash your hands with soap after handling the peppers.

1 Chop the onion, cilantro, and tomatoes. Place them in a small bowl.

2 Finely chop the jalapeno and add it to the bowl. Keep your hands away from your eyes.

Utensils

KNIFE

CITRUS REAMER

CUTTING BOARD

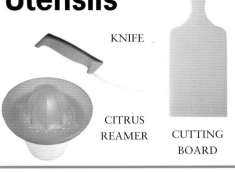

3 Squeeze the limes, then pour the juice into the bowl with the tomatoes. Be careful to remove the lime pits, which are very bitter. Add the salt and mix well.

4 Place salsa in a serving dish. Serve with chips or as a sauce. The salsa will taste best if made the day before.

Ingredients

1 onion

½ bunch cilantro

2 tomatoes

1 large jalapeno pepper

3 limes, squeezed

½ teaspoon (3 ml) salt

The Day of the Dead

One of the most important festivals in Mexico is the *Día de muertos*, which means the Day of the Dead. This festival is held on November 2. The Day of the Dead combines ancient Aztec traditions with celebrations of the Spanish Roman Catholics who settled in Mexico during the 1500s. The original celebrations were held during the Aztec month of *Miccailhuitontli*, which is similar to August. These festivities were dedicated to children and the dead. Spanish priests moved these celebrations to November so that they happened during Roman Catholic feast days. Today, Mexicans celebrate *Día de muertos* by meeting together in the cemeteries where their relatives are buried.

Bread of the Dead

- 2 cups (500 ml) plain flour
- 2 tablespoons (30 ml) butter, softened
- 2 eggs
- ⅓ cup (75 ml) sugar
- dash of salt
- 2 tablespoons (30 ml) grated orange zest (peel)
- 1 cup (250 ml) olive oil
- ⅓ cup (75 ml) icing sugar

Sift the flour into a bowl. Add the eggs, butter, sugar, salt, and orange zest to the bowl. Stir the ingredients together with a wooden spoon. Knead the dough with your hands until it is smooth and elastic. Cover the dough with a clean cloth for 30 minutes. Afterward, roll the dough into a thin sheet and cut it into rectangular strips. Tie some of the strips into loose knots. Heat the oil in a deep frying pan and fry the strips a few at a time until golden brown. Remove the fried strips with a slotted spoon and place on paper towels. Sprinkle with icing sugar and serve.

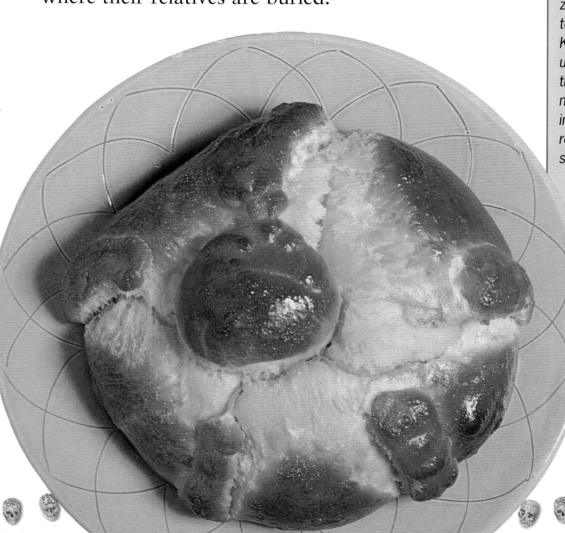

It is traditional to hide a tiny plastic skeleton or skull inside each pan de muerto, *or bread of the dead. It is good luck if you are the one to find it.*

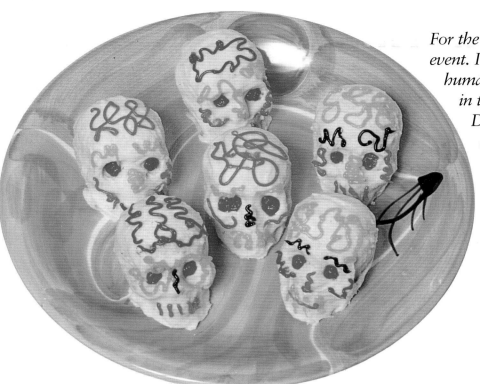

For the ancient Aztecs, death was not a sad event. It was considered another stage of the human journey. Today, when Mexicans gather in their homes or cemeteries to celebrate the Day of the Dead, they eat well, and enjoy each others' company. They also spend time remembering their dead relatives.

During the Day of the Dead, friends and family give one another gifts such as sugar skulls (like the ones above) or other items related to death. People write the receiver's name on the most prized gifts.

The Day of the Dead is celebrated in different ways in the many regions of Mexico. In the southwestern region of Oaxaca, for example, the dead are actually worshiped during the ceremonies. But in most large cities, this holiday is a family day when people get together and share special foods.

Tortillas de harina
Wheat flour tortillas

"Tortilla" is Spanish for "small and flattened." Tortillas can be made from wheat or corn flour. Wheat flour tortillas are more common in the northern states of Mexico. When serving tortillas remember that *"calientitas son mejores,"* which means "they are the best when they are hot."

1 Place the flour, salt, and baking powder into a mixing bowl. Add the shortening to this mixture. Use an electric mixer to blend this mixture together. This process is called **cutting the shortening**. The dough will have a coarse texture when it is ready.

Utensils

- MIXING BOWL
- SPATULA
- ELECTRIC MIXER OR PASTRY BLENDER
- SLOTTED SPATULA
- ROLLING PIN OR TORTILLA PRESS
- SKILLET OR FRYING PAN

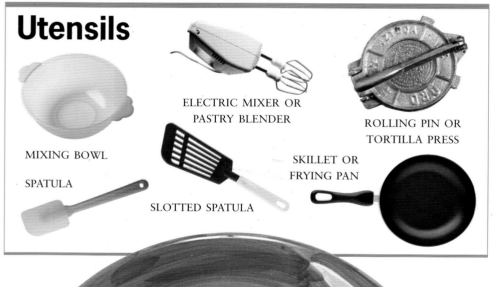

2 Add the hot water to the dough a little at a time. Use your hands to blend it together until the dough is smooth. Put some flour on a clean surface and place the dough on it. Put flour on your hands and **knead** the dough about 20 times. Leave it for 10 minutes.

3 Take a piece of dough about the size of an egg and shape it into a ball.

4 Use a rolling pin to flatten the ball into a tortilla about 6 in (15 cm) wide. Repeat steps 3 and 4 until all the dough has been used.

5 Heat a frying pan to medium heat. Cook a tortilla for about 2 minutes until it starts to turn light brown.

6 Use a spatula and flip the tortilla. Cook for 2 more minutes. Remove the tortilla. Repeat until all the tortillas are cooked.

TIPS & TRICKS

To keep the tortillas warm, put a clean dish towel on a plate. Place the warm tortilla on the dish towel and cover with the other end of the towel. You can also warm tortillas in the oven at 200°F (100°C).

Ingredients

4 cups (1000 ml) plain flour

2 teaspoons (10 ml) salt

2 teaspoons (10 ml) baking powder

4 tablespoons (60 ml) shortening

1½ cups (375 ml) hot water

Arroz Mexicano

Mexican rice

Rice was introduced to Mexico by the Spanish. It has become very popular and is used in appetizers, main courses, and desserts. This rice and vegetable recipe is healthy enough to be served on its own for dinner. If you like hot and spicy food, try serving this with the *Salsa pico do gallo* recipe on page 20.

1 Chop the onion, tomato, and bell pepper. Measure 2 cups (500 ml) water. Set aside the vegetables and water until later.

2 Place a frying pan on the stove at medium heat. Add the oil to the pan and warm it up. Add the rice and stir until it is light brown.

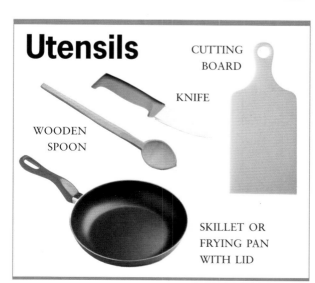

Utensils

CUTTING BOARD

KNIFE

WOODEN SPOON

SKILLET OR FRYING PAN WITH LID

3 Add vegetables and stir until they are tender but not mushy.

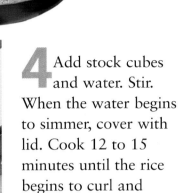

4 Add stock cubes and water. Stir. When the water begins to simmer, cover with lid. Cook 12 to 15 minutes until the rice begins to curl and become soft. Serve hot.

TIPS & TRICKS

Use a long-handled wooden spoon to stir the rice. It will keep the heat away from your hand, and it will not damage the surface of your frying pan. While stirring, make sure that you scrape every part of the bottom of the pan. Occasionally, scrape the sides of the pan to make sure everything is mixed together.

Ingredients

1 onion

2 tomatoes

1 green bell pepper

1 tablespoon (15 ml) vegetable oil

2 cups (500 ml) rice

2 cups (500 ml) water

1 vegetable or chicken stock cube

Frijoles

Pinto beans with tomato and bacon

Beans are **native** to Mexico and are one of the country's most common foods. There are many recipes with beans as the main ingredient. In Mexico, beans are traditionally cooked in large clay pots. These pots give the beans a special flavor. We suggest you use a pressure cooker or a pot with a tight lid. During most of the year you will only be able to find dried pinto beans. These beans require soaking overnight before they are used.

1 Carefully sort through the dried beans. Throw away any beans that are wrinkled or cracked. Pick out any small stones.

2 Place beans in a bowl and cover with water. Soak them overnight. Afterwards, drain the water and place beans in the pressure cooker.

4 Cook for about 1 hour, or until the beans are plump and soft. Check the pot often to make sure there is water covering the beans. Ask an adult to help you when raising the lid.

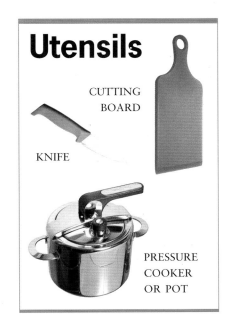

Utensils

CUTTING
BOARD

KNIFE

PRESSURE
COOKER
OR POT

3 Chop the garlic and the bacon and add to the cooker. Add the crushed tomatoes, salt, and enough water to just cover the beans. Cover with the lid and bring to a boil.

Easy refried beans
If there are any beans leftover: fry an additional 4 to 5 slices of chopped bacon. Add the beans and mash. Serve on tacos, **chalupas,** *or as a side dish.*

Ingredients

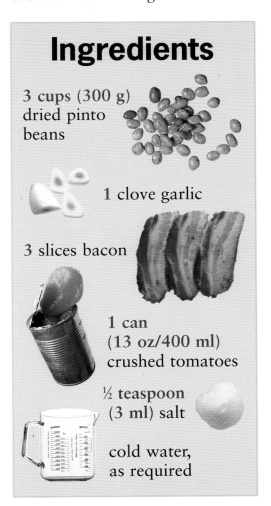

3 cups (300 g) dried pinto beans

1 clove garlic

3 slices bacon

1 can (13 oz/400 ml) crushed tomatoes

½ teaspoon (3 ml) salt

cold water, as required

TIPS & TRICKS

A pressure cooker is a pot with a locking lid and a valve for steam to escape from. Food is cooked quickly in these pots. If you do not have one in your kitchen, just use a large, deep saucepan with a tight-fitting lid. Beans cooked in this type of pot will take about 2 hours to cook.

Tacos

Tacos make a tasty lunch or snack. You can prepare the fillings ahead of time. Make sure you fill the taco shells just before serving so that they stay crunchy. Add *Salsa Pico do Gallo* (pages 20-21) to your tacos for extra flavor. Taco filling also tastes great on top of a *chalupa*. To make a *chalupa*, fry a tortilla flat instead of in a curved pocket.

Ingredients

1 small onion

2 ripe tomatoes

1 lettuce, washed and chopped

1–2 cloves garlic

1 pound (450 g) ground beef

1 teaspoon (5 ml) salt

1½ teaspoons (8 ml) chili powder (optional)

10 to 12 hard taco shells

1 cup (225 g) cooked beans drained or refried beans

1½ cups (375 ml) grated cheddar cheese

Utensils

WOODEN SPOON

CUTTING BOARD

KNIFE

CHEESE GRATER

SKILLET OR FRYING PAN

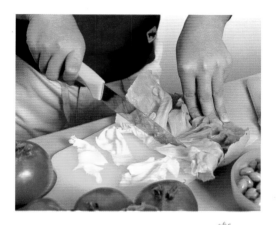

1 Chop the onion, tomatoes, lettuce, and garlic and set them aside.

2 Place a frying pan over the stove on medium heat. Add the beef, garlic, salt, and chili powder to the pan. If you are using cooked beans, add these to the pan as well. Cook and stir until the meat is brown. Make sure there is no pink left in the meat. Drain away any liquid from the meat.

3 Fill the taco shells with meat, beans, lettuce, tomato, and onion.

TIPS & TRICKS

If you cannot find crunchy taco shells, ask an adult to make them for you. Heat 1 inch (2.5 cm) of oil in a frying pan on medium high heat. Place a corn tortilla in the hot oil. Use tongs to fold it over. Fry one side and then the other. Drain the shells on paper towels.

4 Top with grated cheddar cheese. Cover with spoonfuls of spicy *salsa*, if you like.

Churritos

Sweet tortilla fritters

Churritos can be served on their own as sweet fritters. They are also great with vanilla ice cream. If you do not want to eat fried food, you can bake these treats in the oven. Preheat the oven to 350°F (180°C). Cut the tortillas into ½ in (1 cm) strips. Twist the strips and place them on a lightly greased cookie sheet. Sprinkle with cinnamon and sugar and bake in the oven until they are crunchy.

Utensils

SKILLET OR FRYING PAN

SLOTTED SPATULA

KNIFE

CUTTING BOARD

1 Cut the tortillas into quarters. Heat the oil in a frying pan over medium high heat.

2 Carefully place the tortillas in the pan. Be careful! The oil is very hot. It could splatter on your hands and arms and cause painful burns. Ask an adult to help and watch you.

3 Fry the tortillas until they are golden on both sides. Place cooked tortillas on paper towels. Repeat until all tortillas are fried.

4 Sprinkle the tortillas with cinnamon and sugar. Serve while still hot!

When cooking, make sure that the handles of pots and pans do not hang over the edge of the stove. Turn the handles inward so that they will not get bumped. Never leave the kitchen when you have oil on the stove. It can catch fire. If it does, turn off the heat and leave the kitchen at once. Find an adult to help you put out the flames.

These sweet fritters are "deliciosos con chocolate," which means they "go well with chocolate."

Ingredients

4 small wheat flour tortillas

1 cup (250 ml) vegetable oil, for frying

cinnamon to taste

½ cup (125 ml) sugar

Flan

Baked custard with caramel topping

This dessert is cooked in the oven using a technique called **bain-marie**. To cook *bain-marie*, the pan with the food is placed inside a larger, deeper pan that is filled with water. As the water is heated, it creates steam in the oven which is just right for baked custards.

34

Utensils

ELECTRIC MIXER

LARGE PAN
(SHOULD BE MUCH LARGER
THAN THE BAKING DISH)

MIXING
BOWL

1 QUART
(1 LITER)
BAKING DISH

1 Preheat the oven to 350°F (180°C). Spread a thin layer of butter inside the baking dish. Break four eggs and place them in a mixing bowl. Beat the eggs with an electric mixer until they are smooth.

2 Add the milk, cream, sugar, and vanilla to the eggs.

TIPS & TRICKS

When putting things into or taking them out of the oven, always wear thick, protective oven mitts. If the dish in the oven is heavy, ask an adult to help you move it. When you are finished cooking, be sure to clean up the kitchen. Cleaning helps to keep germs out of your kitchen and your food.

3 Beat with the electric mixer until well mixed. The mixture should be smooth and creamy.

4 Gently pour this mixture into the baking dish. Scrape the sides of the bowl to get out all of the mixture. Place the baking dish into the larger pan. Use a cup and fill the larger pan with hot water to come up around the edge of the smaller dish.

Ingredients

butter, to grease the baking dish

4 eggs

1 cup (250 ml) milk

1 cup (250 ml) light cream

½ cup (125 ml) granulated sugar

1 teaspoon (5 ml) vanilla extract

½ cup (125 ml) brown sugar

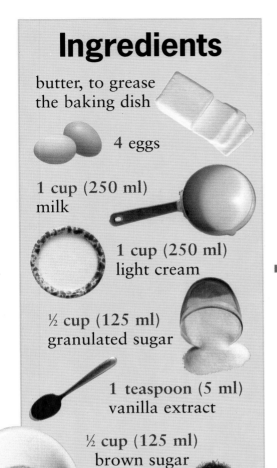

5 Place the pans into the oven. Ask an adult to help you, because the water may spill out. Bake for 1 hour. Place a toothpick into the center of the flan. If the toothpick comes out clean, the flan is cooked. Remove the flan, let it cool, then chill in the refrigerator for several hours.

6 Make sure the oven rack is about 8 in (20 cm) from the top grill. Turn the oven on to **broil**. Sprinkle the top of the flan with brown sugar. Ask an adult to help you place it into the oven. Broil until it is light brown and the sugar starts to melt. Have someone help you remove it from the oven. Serve immediately.

Arroz con leche

Rice pudding

Rice pudding is a traditional Mexican dessert. The pudding can be served chilled or while it is still warm with ice cream. Another way is to cook the pudding until it is very thick. Roll the pudding into balls and fry them until golden brown. Sprinkle the balls with cinnamon and sugar and serve warm.

1 Combine the rice, **evaporated milk**, sugar, and egg yolks in a saucepan over medium heat. Stir.

2 Add the vanilla extract, raisins, and spices. Simmer for 5 minutes over low heat. Remove from the heat.

3 Beat the egg whites with a mixer until they are stiff. Scoop the whites carefully into the rice mixture.

4 Spoon the mixture into bowls. Sprinkle with the cinnamon and place in the refrigerator for at least 2 hours. Serve when chilled.

Utensils

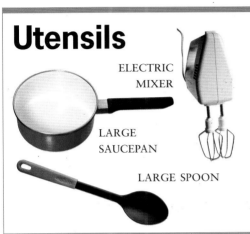

ELECTRIC MIXER

LARGE SAUCEPAN

LARGE SPOON

Ingredients

1 cup (250 ml) cooked rice

GLORIA LECHE EVAPORADA

2 cups (500 ml) evaporated milk

¾ cup (175 ml) granulated sugar

1 cup (250 ml) raisins

3 eggs, separated

1 teaspoon (5 ml) vanilla

¼ teaspoon (1 ml) cinnamon

¼ teaspoon (1 ml) nutmeg

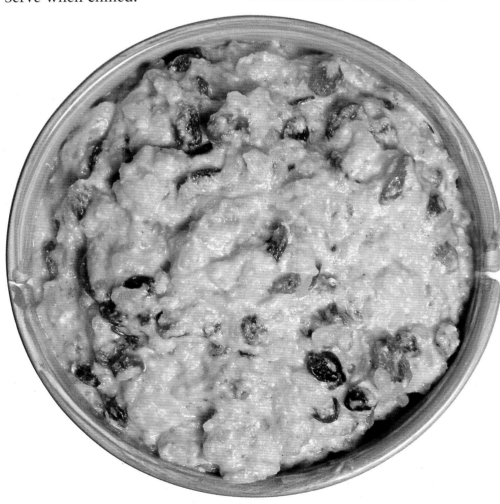

TIPS & TRICKS

If you do not have an egg separator, you can do it yourself. Crack the egg over the bowl. Gently pour the egg into half of the shell without breaking the yolk (the yellow part). Allow the white to slide into the bowl. Repeat until all the yolk and whites are separated. Put the yolks in a separate container from the whites.

Glossary

Abuelia chocolate A brand name Mexican chocolate used for making hot chocolate

Aztecs An ethnic group that ruled much of Mexico before the Spanish arrived in 1521

bain-marie A water bath technique used to gently cook or steam food

beat To mix a liquid or soft paste rapidly

broil To grill food at very high heat

broth A watery soup seasoned with meat, fish, or vegetables

chalupa A tortilla fried flat until crisp

cilantro A herb used in cooking; also known as *coriander*

dice To cut food into tiny cubes using a knife

dissolved When something, such as sugar, disappears into a liquid, such as water

evaporated milk Unsweetened, canned milk that has its water removed by evaporation

frothy Describing a liquid that has been shaken or stirred until bubbles form

garnish To add a portion of food to the side of a dish as decoration

knead The act of mixing and smoothing out dough before it is baked

ladle (n) A long-handled scoop used to serve soups; (v) To scoop a liquid

Mayans An ethnic group that were one of the first peoples to live in Mexico

mince To cut or chop into very small pieces

native Belonging to, or originating from a certain area or country

pesticide A chemical used by farmers to kill insects and pests that eat their crops

separate in cooking, to divide an egg's yolk from its white, both to be used at different stages of a recipe

simmer To cook just at or below a liquid's boiling point

tamales Minced meat packed in cornmeal dough, wrapped in corn husks and steamed

tostados A bite size tortilla fried until crisp

veined To remove the veins from a vegetable such as a chili pepper

Index